For Thomasina and Willow – M. J.
For Fern – R. S.

This is a book about a fox, and it is also a book about light and dark.
As you read this book with a child, you may want to discuss the following concepts:

Light comes from many different sources. Daylight comes from the sun.
Moonlight is light from the sun that has bounced off the moon. Light from streetlights,
flashlights, and headlights comes from electricity. Very hot things may also give off light.

When solid objects get in the way of light, they cast shadows.
Transparent materials (such as glass) allow light to pass through them.
Reflective objects (such as mirrors) bounce the light back to the viewer.

Fox Explores
the Night

Martin Jenkins

illustrated by
Richard Smythe

CANDLEWICK PRESS

Fox wakes up in her dark, cozy den.
She's hungry!

She goes to the entrance and looks outside.

The sun is shining brightly.

There are people around.

Perhaps she'd better wait a while.

She turns around and goes back to sleep.

Fox wakes up again. She's even hungrier now. The sun is going down, it's not as bright, and the people have all gone. She leaves her den.

Now the sun has
disappeared completely.
Fox sets off down the path
to find some food.
She has sharp eyes, but she still finds
it hard to see when it's dark.

A mouse!

But the mouse is
too fast for Fox.

Fox is getting really hungry now.

Perhaps she'll find something tasty by this trash can.

Suddenly she stops. She stares.

Another fox! She steps forward.

The other fox steps toward her.

She steps forward again.

Bump!

Something's coming.
Fox better get out of here.

That was close.

Fox turns down an alley.
Something smells interesting.

She slips through a hole in a fence.
She inches forward.
It's hot and bright!

She's found her supper.
And there in the moonlight is the path
through the trees, leading her safely home.

THINKING ABOUT
LIGHT AND DARK

Can you find examples of different light sources in the book?
Look for sunlight, moonlight, and electric lights.
Stand outside in the sunlight. How long is your shadow?
Stand outside again a couple of hours later. Is your shadow longer
or shorter? Can you figure out why?

Look up the pages to find out more about light and dark.

First U.S. edition 2018

Library of Congress Catalog Card Number pending
ISBN 978-0-7636-9883-6

18 19 20 21 22 23 TLF 10 9 8 7 6 5 4 3 2 1

Printed in Dongguan, Guangdong, China

This book was typeset in Kreon.
The illustrations were done in mixed media.

Candlewick Press
99 Dover Street
Somerville, Massachusetts 02144

visit us at www.candlewick.com